Eat Quite Everything You See

EAT
QUITE
EVERYTHING
YOU SEE

poems by

Leslie Adrienne Miller

Graywolf Press

SAINT PAUL, MINNESOTA

Publication of this volume is made possible in part by a grant provided by the Minnesota State Arts Board, through an appropriation by the Minnesota State Legislature, a grant from the Wells Fargo Foundation Minnesota, and a grant from the National Endowment for the Arts. Significant support has also been provided by the Bush Foundation; the Lannan Foundation; Marshall Field's Project Imagine with support from the Target Foundation; the McKnight Foundation; and other generous contributions from foundations, corporations, and individuals. To these organizations and individuals we offer our heartfelt thanks.

Published by Graywolf Press
2402 University Avenue, Suite 203
Saint Paul, MN 55114
All rights reserved.

www.graywolfpress.org

Published in the United States of America

ISBN: 1-55597-365-5

2 4 6 8 9 7 5 3 1
First Graywolf Printing, 2002

Library of Congress Control Number: 2001096559

Cover Art: Nicolas de Staël, *Le grand concert*, 1955,
huile sur toile, Musée Picasso d'Antibes
© 2001 Artists Rights Society (ARS), New York / ADAGP, Paris

Cover Design: Christa Schoenbrodt, Studio Haus

Acknowledgments

Grateful acknowledgment is made to the editors of the following publications in which these poems first appeared:

The American Poetry Review: "Trying to Reach My Young Lover
   Before His Feet Get Too Cold"
Crab Orchard Review: "Photograph of People Dancing in France,"
   "Sundays When Their Laps Were Full of Light," "Trading Love
   Stories in Installments, Ruined Amphitheater, Provence"
Crazyhorse: "Clarté: Staël at Antibes," "Police Work," "He Thinks I'm
   Making a Monster," "Intimate Apparel," "Panorama Place"
Critical Quarterly: "*La Création*"
Ekphrasis: "Portrait *Trouvé*"
Great River Review: "Cautionary Tale"
Gulf Coast: "One Moon View of Puget Sound"
Harvard Review: "Prévert's Peaches"
Mississippi Review: "After an Evening with Mickey Rourke, I Pick
   Up Petrarch"
The North American Review: "Véritable Laguiole"
River Styx: "On Being Asked What Compels Me to Keep Making Art"
Seneca Review: "The Actual Heart"
Southern Indiana Review: "No-Man's-Land"
Spoon River Poetry Review: "Three Begonias," "Imagining Myself with
   Child at Forty"
Sycamore Review: "The Lyric Impulse"
Water~Stone: "*Nature Morte*"

"Portrait *Trouvé*" and "The Many Faucets of Love" also appeared in
The Loft McKnight Awards Anthology, published by the Loft Literary
Center, 1998.

The author wishes to thank Hawthornden Castle International Writers' Retreat in Lasswade, Scotland, the Loft Literary Center, the McKnight Foundation, the Minnesota State Arts Board, and the University of Saint Thomas for their generous support during the completion of this book. This book is for all those who gave me refuge, Hannelore Jüterbock, Jutta Frantzen, Jeffrey Hessing and Jennie Dallery, Corinne Maynadie, Olivier Legrand, and above all, Heid Erdrich, who kept me tethered to home.

Contents

What is at stake is an adventure of vision.

JACQUES DERRIDA

The Anarchist

Only on the way to evening does the sea
begin to come back, the hills between here

and there, which were sharply green, attentive
all day, go blue. Great blots of shadow appear

where Aleppos shelter succulents. At evening
the harbor too comes back, its white blear

warming with yellow, each roof slant and wall
stripe clarifying into the somewhere they are

but weren't in our minds all day because the light
doesn't allow the eye that far in summer.

Little silver fish of a plane sliding east,
boat flecks unfastened from their distances

materialize with evening. Possible roads
emerge, meander, disappear; windows flare

like stolen squares of the way the water will,
at last, return. We will never see people on the coast,

not at this reach, but we see what the light does
to them, which is more than they know of us.

We are less than shadow to them, crouched
on the south side of a mountain. We lose the light

before they and are safe. The promontory
of our village is a prow, and we echo the sea

so it cannot detect us. Our noise. Our bread
breaking. The damp stones inside our houses

silence all sunder and flux. Those who live
down by the sea return to it at night, and we study

their spilled light, imagine their music, which is better
than actually hearing it. We know it is impossible there

also, cool water standing aside for the Pastis. There too
they love the cloud rising in the glass. At that edge

they drink to bring on the sadness more sweetly;
here we drink to fend it off. Either way, the body

of water is one of the oldest in the mind. Believing
begins near it. There color was born and given

its beautiful names: *Cobalt, Cadmium, Cerulean,*
Napoli Yellow, Hansa, Ocre, Nuance de Bleu.

The houses could be rocks, the rocks could be roads.
The boats could be doubts or birds. That's what

art is for: to remind us that we have not seen
what we remember having seen. If I say

Mediterranean to you now, all this will freeze
into *azure,* and you will lose the richly actual

to mere knowledge, the terrible stillness
that keeps the eye from going too far.

What would there be in a story of happiness?
Only what prepares it, only what destroys it can be told.

ANDRÉ GIDE

Insolence

Josephine spreads her *Star Wars* puzzle on the plank table
filling the kitchen of the flat in a walled medieval city
on a spur above the Var. There Josephine perches shirtless
and gleeful among the tall adults whose attention she knows
she'll get. Her father tells her she must do her puzzle elsewhere,

gives her soft cheese and bread, warms her milk, but Josephine
will work her puzzle here, and if her father tells her no,
all the better. She can wail and stamp her feet on the ancient
tiles, threaten to tell *Maman,* who will scoop her beautiful,
surly child to the rich, small cage of her own arrogance.

This is a girl so perfectly made that her mother
may never again throw a pot or mix a glaze to stopper
her longing for satisfying shape. We were all such
beauties once, hoarding our right to insolence for when
it wouldn't be so easy to squander — spread like a puzzle

across the table where six adults are about to dine. The candles
gutter and spit with Josephine's tantrum, and though I know
so little French I cannot follow dinner talk, I know *insolence*
in French and English is the same elegant word for privilege
we accumulate in childhood and parcel out over all our lives

to save ourselves from mediocrity. The raspberry tart,
insolent too, spills its ruby glaze against gold paper
as Josephine, naked and squirming, twines her uncle's neck,
splays her fine black child's hair across his chest. He hugs
her lightly, fights to keep his fondness from rising to desire.

Josephine's fret is the only French I understand completely,
her threats and pursed lips, desire at its purest, clearer
than the circles the adults wind in air to help me get their jokes.
I listen watching mouths, catch at random words like sparks
as they dissolve, and fix on Josephine's mother's face,

read the fine articulation of her collarbone, her olive
nape, the vein between her temple and her ear, a fluent
blue. She laughs, looks at me because the laugh,
if not her words, is mine. Moans of pleasure over food,
the wine they push my way, the *are-you-happy-in-your-silence?*

smile, these I follow, and all the stately cognates,
impudence and *arrogance, impatience, apologie.*
Later when we step into the cobbled street where cloying jasmine
slips its girlish breath, I understand at once. *Extravagance,*
Josephine's uncle whispers, carving me a sprig because he knows

how this unruly scent will spook my sleep, the red *tarte aux fruits*
glitter, and the few French words I do know, *fille, fleur, souci,*
stain my tongue like that red glaze its paper lace. *Extravagance,*
I say in English, though it's not so sweet. I'm a woman going
under in the dark, and I don't mind as I once did.

There is a certain kind of love I could now live without.
I stand on tiptoe for the parting kisses at which I'm still
inept, brush my lips on collarbones and hair:
the kiss, almost a word, almost a scent, sneaky
and heartbreaking as Josephine's lantern of ribs. *There,*

he says, *I lived as a child,* and we lift our eyes to a dark
but open window on the street. We were all permitted insolence
once; the world made us so, that we might be loved even
as we spent ourselves in tears and fits. Josephine. As if
her name could save her from a less than legendary life,

as if her name could hold her beauty like water in a glass,
permit her every tantrum, long enough to pass her into love
as patient as her father's. Mother presses child's slowing sobs
against her throat, says *anything child, anything my petite,*
you want, smoothing the blue pool of her skin,

adoring the child's violet nipples, so indistinct they might
be faded drops of wine spilled on the thin paper
of her chest, and not the inevitable clocks, *petite* Josephine,
the tiny, terrible clocks that will one day, and then always,
tell aloud the lateness of the hour in your heart.

Photograph of People Dancing in France

It's true that you don't know them — nor do I
know what I wanted their movement to say
when I tucked them in an envelope with words

for you. I thought it was my life caught
in a warm night. I believed myself loved
by the wan and delicate man you see dancing

against the drop-off behind them all. But you
can't see that they are on a mountain, that
just beyond the railings is a ravine, abrupt

and studded with thorn, beyond it, a river,
dry bed of stone that, by the time you take
the photo from the envelope, will have filled

with green foam of cold torrents from high
in the Alps. This is France, you think, as you look
at the people dancing, but there is nothing of France

visible save one branch of a tree close enough
to catch in their hair. I could tell you that by the time
you see this picture, the young girl with the long jaw

launching her bared navel at the lens will have bedded
the man you're afraid of losing me to. There is food
on the table, French food, and so more beautiful for that,

green olives in brine, a local cake in a paper lace,
sliced tomatoes that look in the flash like flesh
with their red spill of curve and seed. I could tell you

they grew not twenty meters from the table
where you see them, that I picked them one day
with the small woman who bares her breasts

in this photo because she is about to leave us
and doesn't know any other way to say she is sad.
They're alive is all you'll say of the scene, which

is to say you feel you're not. It is November
by the time I've thought to send you the photo,
by the time I feel myself ready to part with the image.

By then, the woman of the manifest breasts has left us,
and the one with the dark eyes who loved her
has darker eyes. Very soon after this dancing stopped,

the man with the hollow cheeks took the girl
of the ripe navel into his bed because he, like you,
is so afraid of dying, he invites it daily, to try him.

The girl's last lover was a boy on heroin in Cairo
with the possible end of them both asleep in his blood,
and now too in the blood of the lover I wanted

to save. Because you are married to a woman
who insists on wearing her dead sister's clothes,
you understand that while I am not in this picture,

I am in this picture. Know that I need never see it again
to see: the incessant knot of the girl's navel is a fist,
an oily wad of sweet-sour girl flesh, a ball of tissue

I twisted and crushed all of that evening, and since.
You refuse to remember her name, or his, because you want
to be my lover again, and the others must be kept

abstract. *They were alive* you say again, not more,
because the heart is nothing if not a grave. You want me
because your wife holds out her familiar wrist to you

in the terrible sleeve of her dead sister's dress,
because I reach for the gaunt cheek of the man
who worships at the luminous inch of belly on the girl

who lifts her arms from the body of a boy none of us
will ever know in Cairo, the girl, who dead center
in the photo, lifts the potent, mocking extravagance

of her flash-drenched arms, and dances for us all.

Nature Morte

A small scorpion kicks, caught in a spider's web
over the desk where I am expected to write
as many great things as possible with the gifts of time
and this famous light. Somewhere my mother has read
that lavender repels scorpions, and she advises me
of this in a letter, as if it were a tip for removing blood
from a fine lace, blood she knows I would otherwise leave,
as I do the scorpion, to rust into a souvenir.
Perhaps she has also read that lavender opens the taps
of male desire — but that, she keeps to herself.

The scorpion hangs here exhausted, the elegant comma
of its tail rooted, pincers open, its fringe of legs spilled
in air. It will take days for the quiescence the spider
desires — her splayed limbs slight, and crooked as scratches
or the invisible joints of a skeleton's unlocked knuckles —
but rhetorical as the long muscle-wrapped arm that reaches
for God on the domed chapel ceiling, one finger fully extended
with the knowledge that what it reaches for is obtainable.
In one of the scorpion's surrenders to languor, the spider
ascends to him gently — I've no idea what she intends —

this being a foreign country, and I here in the woods with
no library or book to tell me whether she'd like him dead
or simply alive but paralyzed. She moves to the still point
of the tail's end, where she sketches thin descriptions
of the deadly part — she's so light in her hunger,
he doesn't seem to know she's there until she's on him.
The web, designed for balance so true, stillness and movement
are one, gives as he curls his spine, pincers and tail spired
above his back, the free legs treading air and rocking them both
— though lightly, because her web, after all, is a soft place.

I don't have to tell you how much I'd like her to have him,
how I admire the bright strings of glue she's strapped
on his corded segments, every bead of his bulk and swagger.
She's got his right pincer wrapped in her opal gauze,
and the stinger. She makes her patient runs down
the invisible ladder of her hunger and throws another
rope around his amber hind leg, pins it to the arch
of his torso. He's strung up like a puppet, the free
pincer clasping the air with its tiny tongs, trying to clip
the cord on the other, but every time he touches himself, he sticks.

It is still possible that the spider will squander three days
and all her threads on the scorpion, then, that I,
forgetting her, might simply close the flimsy curtain
over my desk on which she's built her web. If I were
to take a lover suddenly. One simple sweep of cloth across
the pane, a gesture to satisfy my hunger rather than hers —
and they'd both be on the floor, he running, trailing
her broken threads and missing the use of any of his eight
legs still glued with her sap. It might have been easier for her,
were it a fly, a mosquito, but no, it is this — this monster

which looked yesterday like luck, and today like possible
catastrophe. The foolish scorpion has lifted his free left arm
to pinch the wire that holds his right, and now, that one too
is glued. By morning he's stopped thrashing, strung up
by the end of his tail alone. She's unwrapped the mitt
of gauze from his pincer, touched it lightly to the other.
Though he's not dead. Nor does it matter now if and when
he does die: it's the shape she's made of him that graces me,
a gesture: the beads of his tail, the blue bow of his back
and tiny amber bubbles of his underparts — she's turned him

into a rosary let down from the hand bead by bead,
still warm with the pressure of prayer.

A Whole Bunch and a Long Time

That's what you saw in her eyes, that old witch,
need, who made you swoon with want and not
all at once, who made your little chunk heart
cower, take cover, fear to be pressed like a button.

Pure girl, she's all mutinous and floral, hair like gauze
that sticks to your mitts, pools of murk and oil
that swirl. You're seriously dizzy, oh she's a whole
port city of places to be lost, and the turns of her

brim with grinning cats and ruby dark doorways;
if she's a house, the basement stairs are a tongue
you could tiptoe down, but you'd be caught. The twins,
Possession and Obsession, live there, quiet most of the time —

you'll never see them at the breakfast table,
but they bang doors all night, whoop as they shimmy
down the banister on their bottoms, those wild babies
who make your bones quake and powder

if you see them in daylight. Place that feels like home,
rooms that lean on you. Dried roses in every bowl,
ashes of a dead pet, teeth of a former husband, toothbrushes
from all those ordinary nights; rags and gestures —

eyes of anyone who's washed here, who's shed whiskers
and curls in the towels, dropped little pouches of seed
into the plumbing, all the while looking a bit sheepish
about the waste of it — *Sorry,* say his eyes, *sorry babies.*

It's a whole bunch but not a long time. Another
who went off eons ago still can't forget the lace
at the windows, those monkeys and bees climbing
the glass, teasing belief. He hadn't seen the boy coming.

Now he remembers someone in the lawnchair, waiting,
those lilacs frothing on the doorstep, a leaky cooler full,
her sweet sick wads of taffeta and tulle. Now it's spandex,
and the dresses spring like snakes from the depths

when he goes for a belt — smell of someone — who?
Gladioli dripping their lowest blooms before the highest
even think of coloring. Always that noisy bevy of girls,
friends, she said, but too many shredding his psyche

like a ribbon they were trying to curl. Each guest
said of the last: *I don't understand how the others
failed,* and then failed again. There were summer
distractions, trains shaking up the night, fires full

of faces and shapely hands. Most of the guests
were pretty, some smart. Nobody blind. The wind
blew up every skirt she owned, and she kept busy
learning the names of the flora as the landscape

changed its address: phlox, roses large as baby heads,
even frangipani, lamb's ears, more poppies than anything else.
Years were foghorns over water, trains bearing grain,
particular bus stops and cafés with too many kinds of coffee.

Music grew like creeper, inches a day, arias over
the windows, riffs under the floors, horns and strings
making lace of the air, her memory for these, keener
than for kisses and hips. All those footprints in the dew

gone by noon. Everybody came back for a drink
in September, but nobody sat in the deep chair.
She was a moat around their knees, a breeze against
the inner ear, a toy of light crossing the rug. A long time

of hunger and leaves turning, snow and sky wheeling
through its kilo of moods. She'd be bones before the crowd
of princes realized the glass had to come off. She wanted
one of you, ever after, to get up and let the dog out.

She wanted to wash your shirts so many times
they thinned, polished the chairs and highboy to whorls.
She wanted to get to the end of a hundred bars of soap
and seasons and wheels of cheese. She wanted her nose

up against your flesh until it hung on your ribs like a web,
until it smelled old and was old, until you were a dark
beetle of yourself, a rotted rowboat, a dead shoe,
until you were dust, until you were nothing — together.

Convolvulus Tricolor

for Jutta and Corinne

Two women. Easy together in the twilight, and I
third, but taken in like the skittish coonhound,
his doggy capacity for adoration broken

before he came to them. *Six months,* Jutta says,
before his tail went up again. They show me
photographs — the garden before they wrested it

from the mountain's wish to be stony, the dog
younger, the two of them with longer hair,
their *motos,* meals, a tent on a beach. Three

of us now in the beans pulling green cords, filling
a white bowl. Corinne pulls an aloe open, presses
the gum to her wrists, mine. Jutta hands a wand

of zucchini over the wall, comic, shorn of the flower,
long as a horse's prick, all the words for this in French,
German, English. Green, striped, soft skinned. Corinne

will slice it into flat rounds, dollops of sour cream, nests
of cheese. Jutta will lift white cakes of fish into butter,
trim a clove of garlic above the pan. Bean steam.

Bluing of evening. Corinne bends inside a vine, skull-sized
leaves of the zucchini sneaking off into the woods, snips
near each bud so the flowers don't tap out the vine's desire

to bear fruit. The dill already yellow, September a step
away, breath of the river cooling the terraces, sage pouring
ears over the path. Corinne stands up, says soon it will be

wood we're cutting. Hunches back into the vine. I leaf
through the stacks of photos, hungry for their former
joy: one of them on a curve, a gorge angling away,

bright plats of snowshoes in a pile, a splayed
yellow chicken beside a knife. The other naked,
asleep on a blanket beside the Red Sea. Helmets

stacked by a road, lichen, mist. Both of them
on a good morning, tousle-headed, sleepy-eyed
with the pleasure of that time. I pour them each

a glass of wine — want the endless meal of their intimacy
to stay in the frame. What they are is what I remember
seeing through windows at twilight in another country:

more precisely, Baltimore, peering into the yellow squares
of the lowest windows along Charles Street with my then
lover, having something. Not enough. In every window

a life more resonant than ours, heads bowed to meals,
a steaming pot, her feet across his knees, dishes
plunged against a porcelain sink, quiet murmur from

another room, *come now,* one ruby lozenge of wine
left rocking toward stillness in the glass on the sill.
Even broken, their past is a place I want to go again,

complicitous with what they remember, *yes more
photos,* I say, before they divvy them up like cash.
Our worst fears are small enough to travel in pockets,

the brutality of simple purpose. The zinnias now too tall
for their leggy stalks, fall against the path, weighted
with their own drifting heads. Corinne's eyebrows

like birds' wings fly up. She's asking me again
if it's true I don't believe in love that lasts,
that question that loosens a little ting of pain, fork

against a glass, but it wasn't me she was asking.
We've traded all our hope for knowledge, then wanted
back our lavish faith. *Hundreds of years ago,* she says,

these terraces were home to grapefruit trees. It's plain
as bread, the strict economy of women. No one of us
has spoken nor need speak of mothers: what they were

was breath, leverage, space, and what the world was,
was itch, necessity, but not an industry. We are
momentarily water in the twilight, seeping, feeding,

beneath the work of time. The purple blossoms
are only open until eleven in the morning.
Come before then, Jutta says, *and you will see all.*

Clarté: Staël at Antibes

Bending over the ramparts to the teal sea, I want to know
exactly where he fell, if the rocks were splashed with him,

how he met the brink and who exactly found him there,
but they're all discreet, those who make the sum of Staël's life

in words, referring to his "tragic end," the cruelty
of the Southern light, the "final act of non-completion,"

or the "step" he took. Standing at the museum's open windows now,
I see that "stepping" wasn't possible from here, wonder

what he'd say to this — his two rooms on the chateau's highest floor,
downstairs grim Hartung, and the biggest draw, Picasso — two

for whom he didn't really care. I've come, like the sooty smear
of his *Chemin de fer au bord de la mer,* behind Jutta

on the motorbike, wind-tears blotting the sea's hue
like gauze, our motion ripping the sky from the earth

precisely as he saw it: *when I see, I see like no one else.*
The museum matron insists we cannot haul our helmets

through the rooms, though looking out these drop-offs to the sea,
I feel I want it, my bright flinty globe, to hold my head

in place inside the room, which spins with blasts
of light and giant blocks of paint that add themselves

so easily to views from which we've come. Too easily,
some would say, because Staël betrayed the cause of abstract

art, first with bottles, then with nudes, fish and bread, then his failure
to resist rousing blue-and-red-clad backs at a football match

in *Parc des Princes.* He moved toward the shapes
of the world even as he knew it was a betrayal. *Which*

window was it? I keep wanting to know. *Was it even this house?*
The brochure doesn't say, and Michelin fails there too.

Couldn't have been despair, couldn't have been "chosen
destiny" or "an act of nobility." Had to be wonder that sent him

out against the color of the water like a blade against impasto,
mere days after the concert in Paris returned him to Antibes

obsessed with the black wedge of piano squatting under the pressure
of so much undiluted red, the instrument stumbling like a mad dog

through the spill of sheet music toward the great gold bass
bleeding its amber warmth over the bleached floor.

Does it matter now that I can say what I see: piano
or dog, bass or pear? The light was brutal here.

Is. The ethereal lives in the familiar heart of the real.
There's such a thing as too much color: *burning*

up the retina of one's eye on the 'shattering blue'
as Char puts it, one ends up seeing the sea red

and the sand violet. And I would do anything
to be near someone trying, this way, to die.

The Lyric Impulse

At the party of painters I'm asked to read a poem,
though play with words is suspect in a room
of hands that rather only color, smear and scratch

whatever love or ill they bear their worlds. Still
an undertow of vengefulness is audible to all,
our art a skill with which we force ourselves

to profit by the detritus. Supposed savants,
the willful mad — our lot reducible to this:
fear and faith so tightly intertwined

we're each a random palette, can't tell
what we've made from what we merely
lived. None of us is capable of conversational

ease, even with accoutrements of fest,
music, trays of olives, sugared cakes.
We've cooked all day for this — traded clothes,

mugging for the lens. Still, we're socially inept,
unsure of how to use a body after life inside the eye.
One of us paints only trees and concrete blocks

because the human figure turned on him, volatile
and lush. He made her into fresco, mountain, stone,
before the swells came back. Were they thighs

or pearly walls? The hospital where pigeons
saved him from the multitude of pills?
There's a beast in me I dislike too —

that's why he turns to me, when the party
pushes shadow shapes against us both,
eats a date, and aims his sugared finger

at my head. *That mind,* he says as if he's been
inside. He pulls it back, the hand that almost grazes
hair, hand that knew me once, tried the buttons

of a summer blouse, drew back from certain
wreckage, and now denies it all. Though others
see, register the shock, velocity of rage.

I say, because we have an audience for cruelty now,
what I've said before, this time with my slam
of turned back, *at least a dozen ruined men,*

you among them, down around that fire.
He shakes his hand to show he feels the burn.
Do you ever, he asks, winding his open palms

as though he'd wrap his head in gauze,
write real love poems?

Trying to Reach My Young Lover
Before His Feet Get Too Cold

Writing my name twenty-two times, I think of you
writing my name in the silly frame of *love*

yous. My cursive is loopy, archaic, a lost art,
and you suspect you were never in the subject

position, so you've given up the ghost on the catbird seat,
and you know I could write everything you're afraid of,

and that too, you're afraid of. You blithely tossed
my name into the tiny pulses of l's and o's. Could I

have stopped you, would I have *ta-ta*-ed you before
you sent the photograph? Tall drink of a kid in a pale

tutu, deliberate shadow cupping your jaw on a day
you were screaming with fiasco, I offer you

gravity in an envelope from Indonesia, patience
from a spring in Missouri, and that bewildered flock

of shady lovers, a lesson in courtly love, a handful
of words in languages you don't want to know.

I've bid my bones dance too hard for you, boy
of my heart the blue moon brought and took off

in all of one day — but not before I got you as image:
a man reduced to a boy parading as a girl, wrapping

himself into the fleshy envelope we call *fetal position,*
all your straight bones in the inevitable knot.

Traveler's cheques, of course, why else would one
sign away so many loops and angles. The point of the pen

is that I'm buying money with my name on it
for the trip to you, and I'm bringing Keats on a string,

Pope on a stick, Wordsworth on ten dollars a day.
You're still talking about sex, though the weather likes to taunt

us that nothing stays pretty. You've taken the old doctor to heart,
his long poem of letters and declarations you imagine neglected.

No one your age is reading it. Eliot's a bore, and Dickinson's
hip for the hundredth time. Bitterness is a nice touch,

but only a pinch or the rosemary will be overwhelmed.
Trucks grind their gears hard below my window

at this moment, this confluence of sound, weather, signs
and time, which is part of what we call a *day.* And it's

different now that you are. My dear, I'm down to bones,
bones only for you. From here on out, it should be poems,

poems only for you. You've just discovered *giving up
the ghost,* though you think it means dying. It doesn't,

I've used it for years: the *ghost* is merely an elusive
project, difficult and wearying, something one hasn't

enough burning or breath to see through to an end.
I'm your ghost, dear, your skeletal girl, your woman

on the edge of middle age, your cliché, your impossible
touch, your new baby of the mind. I'm conjured and injured

and not about to die of it. Think of it, the malice I could bear
you, the way I might wear you as long as I live —

You could be my blue boutonniere from a long-ago year,
dried and beribboned, faded and faddish. Oh honey pie,

can you rise above your pond-green Gap shirt, Boss belt
and Bean jacket? I'll lend you a string tie a little wadded

from the barrel I found it in. I'll give you no more stories,
though, than what you've got, summer light dazzling a page,

little chokes of lightning in a dull sky. We're going
everywhere fast — and you're coming with. Ten times

on the twenties, twelve times on the fifties — that's still
how it's done. At my age, heartbreak's hardly what

we die of. Snide remarks heal any wound, believe me.
I'm full of *whatdidya expects* and 18th-century quips.

Love it or leave it, but don't watch too long. It's a dance
that burns the poor soles of your feet. They're black and cold

already — like the old trance dancer's toes. He can't
shake his trance as the lights come up and the tourists

move in with their murmurs and cameras. His pony's a stick
with a raffia mane, snubbed by sparks. The younger ones can't

do the solo dance on coals, but they're good at the Kechak chants —
they're the monkey army who perform in perfect franchise,

all boys with red frangipani blossoms stuffed over their ears.
It's Bali after all — and a good hundred German women

in brand-new *sarongs* comb their damp hanks of hair in rooms
open over rice paddies. They wait for the end of the Kechak dance,

for the boys to return in their crisp, white shirts, *destar*-wrapped
brows and long batiks. They'll come with bamboo trays

of tea and sure fingers into lamplit rooms where desire
is simply a sweet dish, a prickle of breeze in a hot spot:

yes, no, come, go, here and there, gecko and *clove,*
who needs more words when the body's so fluent?

If this is a ghost, why does it pack its bags so carefully —
clean underwear, maps, and all of the music you recommended.

There's a flask of grief in here somewhere too. And sweetie,
if you can find it, I might let you live. You're this missing poem

in the book on the absence of men and the presence
of women in postmodern life. You have to know that everyone

who's anyone has always already said, *Hurry up please, it's time.*

After an Evening with Mickey Rourke, I Pick Up Petrarch

Much beautifully filmed butchery, Cimino's Rourke,
a Polish cop who cleans up Chinatown, drug lords,
New York, and all this, mind you, dubbed in French
so I wake with wads of novel rudeness in my mouth,
pick up Petrarch to wash it out, read the lot
front to back: Francesco's "Letter to Posterity,"
If only I lived well, it matters little how I talked,
the sonnets, odes and canzoniere. My brain still
quaffs the residue of last night's handsome villain,
that slightly fey, freshly scrubbed, Indo-Chinese man,
who I remember lovely from *The Lover.* In either
case, I was in search of something to distract me
from my teched romantic bent; an overdose of romance
usually cures it, a dozen Neoplatonizing sonnets,

stock paradoxes, the "either sentimental or simply
topographic" catalogue, those "literary pigeonholes"
I can't resist. Repetition, recognition of the types,
gives a certain comfort, even smugness. I've only
rudimentary French, but quite enough for cop films,
thrill to strokes of lively action (many murders) in limited
vocab: *putain* and *merde, trou du cul,* and *enculé*
none of which *Larousse* defines, all of which
I've heard aloud more often than the lovely Latinates.
Twenty words will do for understanding
when the situations speak. Bloody corpses, winning
smiles fill the blanks. Mickey's got his Laura too — skinny
Chinese girl, rich and spoiled, fantastic naked silhouette
against the luscious *noir* of New York's rotten night.

Ah, *The mind is stagnant where sorrows lurk and smart.*
She makes him feel his Polish roots, and he drops trou
in record time, recounting all the ways he hates her (*sweet,
lovely foe*), wants her, takes her on the second try,

walking fully dressed (all tweedy) into her bubble bath.
Of course, they've made him blond for this,
Hollywood and me, we can't resist
a fair *and* winsome asshole, cheer him on.
I watch it with a charming Frenchman who sees no
racist motivations here, is busy lusting loudly
for the Oriental gal, as I enjoy the oily grin and gritty
pocks of our pug-faced hero, Vietnam vet Romeo.
My French friend likes the blood, the Chinese thugs
slaughtered and afloat in noodle sewage underground.

I miss, of course, the finer complications of the plot,
elaborate logistics of the all-out war between the cops
and mob, but recognize the usual narrative arc:
the hero's partner greased before the end, his tedious,
unhappy wife, as well, so he can grieve, as Petrarch
would have us know: *hope is incredible to the slave of grief,*
(and Mickey's grief is copious but mercifully short).
These thirties translations of our troubadour are not unlike
a movie script, the twenty-odd most useful fleet
and facile words that consummate in plastic iambs:
the *'neath*s and *yore*s, those *conquer'd oft*s that bother
not at all, the way the *fuck*s in French are rather
for the rhythm's sake, lust being what it is, vicarious,
hilarious, a function of the breath, and not, *O Love,* the heart.

Police Work

I was careful about everything but my body: I gave
my legs to the bulldog's jaws, my hair to the bad
weather, my toes to scorpions under the sink,
everything else to a few rare women who were worth

knowing well. But my mail disappeared. One day also
the garden table walked away. Went to a party to which
I was not invited. There was sun enough to cook eggs
on the stones, and everything I grew wore yellow spots.

Now and then possible rescues offered themselves,
and, believe me, I tried to return all calls, but the teeth
of the wheel turning were tiny. When the mistral finally
stopped, the lily gave out one more white cup. Saws

and lawn mowers began their prestos, and I ate chocolate
generally at six, waited for the light to finish itself
in the direction of the village where tourists and thieves
do not reach. The moon, as anywhere in the world,

was confusion's accomplice. Only the Americans
were guileless enough to tell what they had dreamed.
Pine sap slipped from the cut limbs above me, looked
like cum on my black jackets, though when asked

what it was, that dim white spot, a gesture answered
better than the word. There were imperialists with whom
to reckon, a minor princess who had no children
so took a childlike husband, randy and devoted to mirrors.

I knew too much and was tolerated only barely.
A big stick was necessary against the hounds, and often
my happiness annoyed them. Also my sadness,
completely unjustified and peculiar to my people,

was unattractive. I read dozens of bad novels,
consoled myself with cold hot dogs and Beethoven
which reminded me of my father on the basement
toilet, "Ode to Joy" cranked, my mother escaped

to her garden. And you whose letters never arrived,
I thought of you daily and read everything
you wrote by default. I had admirers among the locals,
and it was thrilling, because forbidden, to lie in the sun

half naked. Tomorrow they will come for the chairs,
next week for my notebooks and lotions. Now thieves
are blooming in the streets of Nice, says the flirtatious
gendarme, lifting his weapon from its hard case at his hip,

a black coil of telephone cord tethering it to his torso.
He's beautiful, unusually blond for a Frenchman, and sure
as he flips the chamber out, spins, drops the bullets,
harmless as coins, into his palm, to offer the cold tool

to us, two tipsy women. He has watched our faces
through the whole of the 99-franc menu, guessed the foibles
we've traded in our patois of four botched languages.
Now he's ready to make us giggle, to make me reach

over the warm pear slumped in chocolate. He's ready
to make us laugh out loud above her fat half of pineapple
drenched in Cointreau, the champagne going quiet in our
glasses. He's pleased and blushing when we finally reach

for the weight and wonder of it, his prodigious handful of gun.

He Takes Back His Adagios

When it's over, the arc of his rage, the flailing
spate of brutal epithets and spitting, I'm reduced
to weakened knees, but the knot in my gut loosens
in relief. He didn't take the garden apart, or fell

the three creamy cups of my calla, stamp the orange
ice plants down, or rip the jasmine from its slender threads.
He did take back his garden tools, the handsaw, ax,
and hooked machete, the dented spade, then seized

his stack of favorite music. He got the Bernstein, Ravel too,
and all the frail adagios, so sickly sweet I only played them once,
but when he's gone, I see Gorécki's left behind, "Symphony
of Sorrowful Songs," and marvel at his leaving *that*.

Snake, he called me, *snake,* and *fucking scheming womens* too.
I stand amazed in the wake of it, as if it were not me he saw,
yellow-bellied, quaking, but some other wonder of a monster.
I thought myself incapable of raising so much ire,

a watcher only, one for whom love's sad but hardly stormy:
broken men and crazy ones, mama's boys and nearly gays.
This one swinging garden tools like Hercules
is hardly anything to do with me, so distant,

I forget to think *afraid*. He grabs my notebook,
pen, and flings my books, shakes them in my face,
fucking secrets, lies, you voyeuristic shit. To him
my mind's machine, good at shredding things.

I've never had the thrill of such a rage before, and think
This one's really mine. It pours and pours. I can't believe
I'm standing still. Will he swing that shining hook against
my knees? I don't deserve this anger, but neither can I turn

away. Something in me tingles to it, calls it back.
He goes, he goes, this torturing and tortured thing, away
and up the hill from me, his yellow dog unruffled by the wrath,
tumbling after, stopping when he stops, turning when he turns.

She hangs her whiskered head and offers sorry doggy
eyes. He stands above me on the path where I still
expect the sun at nine tomorrow morning, will glory
in the way it fills the curving beds I've gouged

from this hill's stony heart with the very tools
he's brandishing above. I tried to love this crazy fool
once upon a time. He turned from me, diffident
and loath. Something in me panicked him,

an even-tempered distance that incited him to fits.
Now I watch this Oedipus stumbling through the final act,
plucking at his mask of bloody ripped-out eyes. I've watched
because it healed me to see. Rage I couldn't make,

but also couldn't fail to understand, unfolded there,
a carpet at my feet. I step up to the stage
when the fallen king bellows for his daughters,
not his sons, to witness how he's gone ballistic,

threatens, spade aloft, snatching back adagios.
He's right, to call me *snake,* the way I lie in wait,
for the world to come within my range, the way
I'll swallow my mouse whole when it arrives,

take it kicking, without a cry, without a drop of blood,
exactly when it moves, proves itself alive.

La Création

Now and then we scruffy artists get an invitation to return
to the decorous world. Tonight a concert, treat of Haydn
in Monaco's birthday-cake cathedral, to which we rise
resplendent in our borrowed evening clothes through the famous
hunk of rock in starship elevators from the parking garage.

We've been invited down from mountains just beyond the pale,
hope for glimpses of the princess Antoinette. We've spent
a week in scrounging up the proper shoes and skirts,
cracking jokes about the millionaire we'll carry off. Now here
he is, riding up with us, cordial, clean and somehow meek.

He makes us feel bratty, a little out of place. We join the sea
of gabardines and silks pushing gently through the nave,
bristle at our cheap seats in the back. Ignore our linty wools,
our collective scent of woodsmoke, mildew, *eau de dog.*
Before us lies a firmament of impeccable stitching,

the magnificent tints and sweeps of pampered hair,
none of it done at home on rainy days. We whisper,
gossip and gawk as the chorus files in, unaware
we reek of turpentine and ink, last night's fish
and unwashed sheets, crane to see the orchestra

but cannot find the violins behind the mass
of fur-clad backs. One of us is sick with hepatitis C,
has timed his daily shot so as not to be just now in fits
of fever, cramp, and all attendant angers. The cruel work
of healing is costing him a year, three shots a week and all

his nerve. As soon as music reaches us, he can't contain
himself, must comment on this *évocation du Chaos originel*
and flattens palms against the air to show there's not
enough attack. The conductor's hands are limp as fish,
the violins too checked, the orchestra held back.

The angels are too loud, the flutes and oboes drowned.
A painter on the other side of me agrees and frowns.
She played the violin quite well when she was young,
and now at least, she'd like to have a better view
but we're too far to see much more than the crowns

of Uriel and Raphaël. By the time we get to *verdure,*
fleurs, fruits, parfums, a man one row ahead has had it
with our fidgeting critique, turns and slices at the air
as if he's chopping off a head. I close my eyes and pray
the painter on my right, given to fits of rage, won't fly

into one now. Me, I think I'm good at keeping still
until a tickle in my throat sends me into fits of cough.
I close my eyes and try to think of something else —
the models, makes, and colors of all my exes' cars.
By the time the deity's begun to make the stars, the sun

and then the moon, my eyes are running with the effort
to suppress my hack. My face is red, my throat a knot
of phlegm. The painter on my left hands me prehistoric
cough drops melted in their wrappers, stuck with flecks
of loose tobacco, hairs and bits of paper. Then looking

serenely up at Christ, who isn't necessary yet, but floats,
ready in his gold mosaic above our heads, I suck the saving
drop and wonder when it was that all the vivid details
of my childhood disappeared. M. Puissant is thinking how
he'd rather be at home, remote in hand, Rambo tossing thugs

across a room, Rocky punching out another oily brute,
but for now the drums will have to do. Because the making
of the animals begins an hour in, creation seems interminable,
the fishes and the birds swimming and singing while we
wonder where on earth we'll pee. When intermission comes,

we run for the two cold toilets *sans papier.* There are no humans
yet, nor has God done the lions, sheep or insects. Love
is still unthinkable, as are the *beauty* and the *dignity*
of being human. We stand around and smile while our patron
waves us into front-row transept seats for the second half.

By now our lipstick's smirched, we're sleepy and a little chilled —
but here beside the drummer and the violins at last, we're rapt,
commence the population of the earth with animals pumping
all our dubiously clad toes to the tune. Cartoon socks, one bad
bright tie, the giant fissure in my hose opening up my thigh,

a row of plastic purses tucked beneath our seats — we've all
engendered something worthy once, believe we can again.
Man gets made and given Eden. The flutes are tickled.
Eve trills on about the *lucky pair,* and I wonder
at the sprinkling of the French verb *louer* through the text.

I think it means *to rent,* enjoy the naughty thought
of God as greedy landlord, but Haydn can't have been
so droll. Of course, it also means *to praise.* Either way
love's been made, creation ends, and human suffering
doesn't yet exist as we drive home through winter dark,

one to his fevers, one to muscles banging on her bones,
one to simple hunger, and for the rest: fatigue, boredom,
vagueness, cramp, the season's flu and cups of tea. All
of us paying out our numbered days to the stingy god
of making something fine again. The mountains to the north

whiten in the night, and here a bit below, rain and bluer woods;
stones hunker into hillsides, and thorn vines dig them out. Our
borrowed shiny shoes are put away or given back, the trees
go still, and some strange bird will scream till dawn, annoy
the dogs and keep us all awake to petty fears. Still we sigh

like sated children now, yawn, pleasure mixed with boredom
being Eden's special fame. We've been the guests of gods before,
and now will not forget what light was in their wine,
how rare their cuts of beef, how pale the floating orchids
in their finger bowls, birds and fish in blocks of ice, and yes,

how some more-than-mortal creature glanced our way but briefly,
after which we lifted silver forks, bright armies of spoons,
and touched the crystal goblet rims. Oh Monaco, forgive us,
please, we couldn't help ourselves. We simply had to rub
those lovely open ovals with our naughty, wine-dipped

fingertips. We had to try to make them sing.

Sundays When Their Laps Were Full of Light

What is this familiar yellow stuff at the glass again
but Sunday's wide gold loops made by two parents,
two children, driving in a blue Buick away from church
to the meal the children always choose:

a baked chicken leg, yams in syrup, milky pudding,
then the long afternoon of the small town. Laps full
of sunlight, they drive past the courthouse, the banks,
the closed Woolworth's. They cross the river on a steel bridge.

For the mother, they drive by every house for sale in the rims
of town, long low houses hugging lazy sun-blond lawns.
The father later drives them past what he likes, fields
where glowing sheaves lean on the light. One of the girls

in the backseat collects the way it falls in her lap, breaks,
falls and breaks again: phone poles go shadow, shadow, shadow,
and trees go shadow, then shadow, shadow, light light light.
They ride in what the parents surely think is pleasure.

The mother wants other houses. Bigger, prettier houses.
Further out. The father would like to hear his music now,
Beethoven which is at home in a stack of plastic 45s,
but this is the middle of the century and of the country

where even on Sunday there is no Beethoven on the radio.
There is a word, once applied to an herb, but now
obsolete, that some would like restored to the language:
anacampserote . . . that which brings back departed love.

Of the two girls in the backseat, only one,
in thirty years, will wonder: Did we lose the word
because we failed to believe, or did we fail to believe
because we lost the word? The other will not

wonder such a thing but have a child and a house
in Kansas that the mother, now grandmother,
wanders with sighs of approval. Carpets thick as grass,
a rumpus room that always gets the morning light.

That which never arrives cannot be lost, is what
the mother would say to the other girl. She would
say, without ever having read Alain, *Desire is far
inferior to love, and maybe, does not even point*

the way to it. The father, after Beethoven, would
not say that, but neither does he know what to do
for his other girl, the one he suspects of never having
loved at all. This is the light, she thinks, that promised

everything in shadows dropped into our laps, lavish light
that mingles what we hope for with what we think we've lost.

Portrait *Trouvé*

My father in the Menil Museum declaring the pile of tires
meaningless. And out loud, so I have to ignore him, run
into the next gallery, pretend I don't know who
that ignorant man might be. Later, we argue in the cramped

kitchenette of my barrio apartment, my ample father
squeezed between the plane of table and wall. Bristling,
pride in his *humble* view of the world. That story
about the miles of country road to school again,

work at thirteen. What wasn't missed in such
a childhood all the more essential in mine.
After all, *I* was sleeping with a painter at the time,
my special backstage pass to mornings in a studio:

dogs milling at the dock door, obnoxious music,
and a delicate sort of man asking me what I see
in his canvas, then obliterating any figment I divine,
the oriental bridge, the geisha leaning toward her fan —

gone while he offers me the watercolor tray, invites
me, finally, to *paint something.* I do a bad fish
since we are living on his terms now. Pretty isn't
pretty anymore, but already, I have words.

Resentment too. When he leapt into the white truck
at 3 A.M., sped off nailing a mailbox, returning
at dawn minus one more headlight, muffler dragging
like an armadillo's ratty tail: suffering made

the difference somehow, and I'd had too much
privilege for that. Mother scratching out her still lives
in the den: charcoals pinned above the sofa until
I was ten, and that temporary reverence for the made

image. Sketches too, before she turned to making
doll pajamas (snaps so tiny clumsy child-thumbs
couldn't make them fast), of my sister, me,
though there was never, so far as I know, any effort

to capture my father. Rather she found him
in a ruined house, the portrait of some anonymous
fellow who looked very like. Took it. Had it restored,
richly framed, hung over the fireplace like an heirloom

and years enough that we all, almost, came to believe
it *was* my father. Even he shaking his head, turning
away from the uncanny resemblance, the well-
executed grays and blacks of his own emerging

beard, hand at the chin, a gesture he affected — but when?
When the portrait came into our house? Or before?
A matter of belief, after all, that he sat for it,
before it. And my mother thinking all the time

how the grandchildren would never know
the difference if we didn't tell. Not counting, at all,
on the oldest daughter's refusal to give credence
to the man leaning into my father, to give birth

to the lie (or for that matter, to a child), the way
my father himself, now bunched up in the bad shadow
of a cheap apartment across the table from this snotty
young woman crossing her legs, turning up her marvelous

distinctive nose (his, of course) at his refusal to find the art,
Art, shakes his head sadly at her remoteness — she who bears,
for one mean moment, no resemblance to any child of his.

Mise en Abîme

We enter, all eyes cast about at once
to identify maker, made, the precious few
who might consume, review the evening's,

order, light, and wine, signature black
stockings, tailored jackets. We know the frame
repeats itself as trick, the icon of the invitation,

beckoning for weeks from local shops, *café,*
patisserie, tabac. Here at last in real oil,
the ur of it, requiring remark. My companions

divide their comments: what can be said (little),
what can be whispered (more), what can be judged
in silence (much). They scan the narrow hall

for safer distances between their voices
and the maker, trader, those like me who come
to simply see. One of my companions will say

the skin is lighted well in all the nudes.
Then, more softly to me, the litany of all
who do it better. The other doesn't answer

and I know she likes much less, is glad
there's nothing good here. Skin should be a
landscape. Outside, rain, the smell of it

brought in on the stones, damp shoulder pads,
large soft breasts pressed into lace and wire.
Cold gold at certain throats. One turn about

the jammed room and we go, leave the requisite wake
of mock graciousness, tiny puff of condescension,
like a prick of sulfur over a struck match.

The abruptness of our going says: 1) the beautiful
has to be ignored, 2) it is not enough to be vigilant,
3) fame is no accident. My companions

are teaching me to cull sublimity from skill,
to cultivate a looking for, rather than a looking at.
One of my companions studies turning up the light

in rust and rubble, Delacroix denied. The other
erases as she makes, yellow silhouettes of the same
mountain *ville* smudged, effaced until three,

two, then one deep stroke plinth to palisade
brings us to familiar urge of shape: *place,*
the should of it being the whole of it.

Three Begonias

Because I was told they'd grow anywhere,
and they did. In the end, they were the easiest
thing to believe, grew well in a stony place
and were bright. When I turned them under,
the spade found no roots. Think of what Joubert
said, *Women believe all they dare is innocent.*

The White One

The garden is nothing but a space
that wants to be, allows itself to be, gives
itself without question or reserve
to the inevitable geometries of arriving.

Today a man is in it, trying to make me believe
in Alexander the Great. He recounts, battle
by battle, love story by love story, a history
he read. I tell him it's legend, not fact,
down to the last whisper of Egyptian cotton
across a stone. Annoyed, he moves
to the Aristotle part. It's winter anyway,
and we are following the white tablets of warmth
in my stripped garden. *You can have Aristotle,*
I say, *but the rest is poetry,* meaning, with
everyone else, not true.

One was the color of berry, one the moon, one fire.
It's not his fault the begonias are gone, he says,
his are finished too. He would have watered them
if he hadn't fallen in love during the dry time.

The Red One

The butcher and his wife are building a temple
to whatever they believe, and the dogs
do not approve. For us, what the butcher makes
is another good story. The pillars of rough

cement end in crooked cones. He calls it art.
We call it the termite mound. The dogs
have a song for it: blood, gristle, bones,
or gristle, bones, blood. We never get that close
but watch the tops of the trees sway as he fells
the woods. He says he understands the cutting
of trees as well as he understands meat.

Once on a beach in Virginia, I weathered a storm
in a tent with a lover whose fear was greater
than mine. I had to make a legend of it.
In the morning the rangers told us we were
the only ones who lasted the night on the beach.
White branches of lightning appeared to consider
the night sky desirable and touched the edge
of the surf. One of the rangers felt the pressure
of a secret wish on his temple: that someone might
be struck down out there. He did not know why
he had such a wish, but since no one else knew
what his blood whispered, he wasn't entirely ashamed.

I held the edges of the tent with the ends of my body,
and my lover held on to me. In the morning,
the beach a litter of tent scraps, even our cooler
gone to sea. No one dead or even hurt. Desire
is nothing if not that: wishing for the end's promise
of drama. I don't know if he was ashamed of his fear,
the one in my arms. We had a long drive back
to the nearest town each afternoon. Scotch
wasn't easy to find in the bait shops.

Wounded men grow no rinds. Wounded women,
rinds, spines and pits. One was meat, one
flesh, the last, the sun about to drop.

Someone said of George Sand: *she ought to love*
others a little more for their sakes, and a little less
for her own. Then it began to rain and the dog
huddled under us. What would grace be
if it were secular?

The Orange One

At the exhibition of *l'art brut,* the mayor
gives a long speech in French and has himself
photographed with a few of the surviving artists.
It seems one had to be certifiably mad
to be included. The museum and the hospital,
in the end, both suspiciously agreeable interior
spaces. Collectors mill about looking for potential.
Dark at the door, half pill of a moon.
If you collect madmen, you needn't be one.

Red rabbit haunches, boar, half a dozen sorts of bird,
beef, pork, deer. Livers of any and all. I have a fever
and the freezers in the grocery at night are a spectacle.

Vats of terrine with sheets of fat. Think
of the butcher and his tiny wife making love in the tent
by the termite mound. They grow two kinds of lavender,
marguerites, bougainvillea on wires overhead.
They are the last on the hill to have anything blooming
in December. Everything still alive they wrap in tents
of white gauze. Where are the shelves of hope?

When should one think of making a list: the names
of all the former lovers? Admit that you did this
one afternoon, and it wasn't easy.

We had a blue plastic house staked deep in the drift
of sand. When the storm came up, we reclined

on two cheap chairs clicked open toward the sea,
cold glasses in our fists, a bowl of olives between us.
They were from another planet, those olives.
I feel sure I was recalcitrant in whatever point
I was making when the sea began to boil.

A barrier island they called it. Edge of a place,
not a place at all. When the strange wind
stops, this much is momentarily clear: turn despair
into anything less than the agreed upon, and it becomes
impotence. Then terror, though it seems possible
that dogs are capable of happiness.

There were three begonias, each a different
color entirely, a scarlet, a dove, a tangerine.
Or a crimson, an ivory, a rust. Their faces
torn and vague even when I bought them. Go on,
accuse me of narrative now, of leaning on the old wall.
It was three in the afternoon, and she was hungry
when loyalty began to matter so much.

In the end that is not an end, I hang wet clothes
over the empty begonia bed. The blue legs
of the trousers and the yellow squares of towel,
stiff, clean, filling with winter light, appear to bloom.
I tell you this because there are things
even people who love you say about you
that you should never hear.

Imagining Myself with Child at Forty

High instincts before which our mortal Nature
Did tremble like a guilty Thing surprised . . .
WILLIAM WORDSWORTH, "INTIMATIONS ODE"

I paw through row on row of black strapless
dresses hung on loops from the armpit seams,
bouclé, swarms of beads, sequins and pearls.

We're looking for holiday clothes for me,
my friend and I, something to cover
the rough beast of my hope concerning

a man, while she pushes her new daughter
along before her and hugs the next in her womb.
I'll need clean toes, dewy shoulders,

the smooth rib of an underwire to hoist
what there are of my breasts. The child
sleeps on through our experiments in accouterment,

the fitting-room floor a litter of pins and tissue.
We finger rosettes of lace, whorls of crushed
velvet, seamed stockings that dash up the backs

of our thighs. At two months, her child
was a tiny clock of bones loose as a cat's
beneath the sack of skin. I couldn't bring myself

to hold her, but touched her toy cage of ribs,
pronounced her nipples *vague.* Now fifteen pounds,
she holds her head, a third of her weight,

like a giant hat with plumes. Tiny blots
of crust drift at the corners of her eyes.
I try a crepe with princess seams, a silk

sheath, a gored brocade. The child naps on
through lingerie and shoes, jewelry and belts,
wakes to watch me swirling in wads of tulle.

More than twenty years my hips have courted
possibility, the days I came of age a storm
of vanishings, and the one child I might have had

is dross. Now my friend, a woman whose mind
I've always envied, is breeding, the angles of her intellect
softened with the effort of one born, another

on the way. When she asks me *what I'm thinking,*
I tuck my bad habits in my black sleeve and smile
as if I'm swallowing angels. *Nothing,* I say

to the three-way mirror, swimming with infinite
versions of the woman I could still become,
though obstinate skeletons in my closet bang

dry elbows and knuckles on the door,
and my regrets, if regrets they are, proliferate
like pillows in close Victorian rooms,

blowzy with busy rugs, swollen armchairs,
and tasseled ottomans, where I languish
in all the camouflage of an invalid buried

in throws. I feign helplessness, hand to temple
thinking, suffering, or just plain sultry.
A pack of hounds, golden-haired and sleek, wait

at my feet for the curls of cold on the sleeves
of the next visitor to bring a whiff of that world
they were born to. They do remember it distinctly,

the extravagant stink of what so recently
was fierce and floating, glistening gristle
and scales, festive blood and flecks of bone,

the crystal air, birds flushed from dry grass,
rodents stirring in moss banks, and oh the preen
and pucker of marvelous fish zipping beneath thin ice.

He Thinks I'm Making a Monster

of him, but he's busy himself making one of me.
Heard it said I called him fickle, likely to plunge
in love with any tree, golden stone, goblin girl,
or better yet, a completely-obligated-elsewhere

anyone. Why should it seem cruel of me to say?
My romantic interest at the moment being fecund
earth itself, borrowed garden, juicy tubers, makeshift
walls of stone and sticks. I grow a witchery

of potent envy, guilt, a little stardust. Disembodied
ropes of muscle, glittering slime, a scalp of luscious,
deeply rooted hair. These we've both allowed to float
above the edge of consciousness, something pressing

a state of dream, not the deepest kind, but those
that come at dawn, those you reach for, begin to twist
until a narrative emerges, those you tinker with in plot
until they're no longer dream but premeditated thought.

We disturb each other, always have, scamper back
to separate lairs and wave our naughty wands
until the story is twisted, rootless, hysterical and sweet,
much changed and fully possessed, hexed, claimed.

Together in the afternoons, we think, each, of ourselves
as benevolent and fair, winsome Glindas waving power
over innocents in ruby shoes. Wisdom, we have some,
but not enough to use up on ourselves. We hand

it round to others easily, a form of generosity which also
has the name of hope. We'll never understand the way the other
makes his monsters or where he got those parts — the convict's
toes, the ballerina's sturdy spine, the rogue's red cheating heart,

but dear, we are ex-lovers, intimacy run amok, can't help
but find old fairy dust hidden in our shoes. This monster
we are making is every bit the dandy, a masterpiece of self-
deception, irony, and blighted trust. Guileless as a toddler,

and too large to ignore, we made him out of what we were
and wanted, did and didn't get. You wanted back your children.
I wanted pretties of my own. Either way he's dangerous,
this offspring of our lust, but he's yours, my dear, yours,

as surely as he's mine.

Intimate Apparel

for my writing group

I'm touched when they bring their house slippers,
leave their salty boots in the hall, don the woolly
assortment. Valerie brings hers in yesterday's blue
newspaper bag; Martha's come in one from a wine shop.
No one is standing on ceremony here.

Rife and confidential as nightgowns or unmade beds,
mine are my conversation with myself, argument
against the prickle of desire, a gift from my sister
I never thought I'd wear, garish colors and plastic soles,
tucked like wads of gauze beneath my folded knees.

When my grandmother was dying, my mother
kept her in mules that matched her robes,
lipstick to match the tangerine gown, propped
in her wheelchair, mad, crying for ice cream, but *done up,*
as my mother said, because she wasn't alone.

I wear my slippers against cold floors, against the necessity
of going out for groceries, flowers or wine, against guests
altogether, against what sort of old lady *I* will be. Against
the noise of my own body. Invariably, someone leaves theirs
at someone else's house — Martha, who drove across the river,

seven miles, to retrieve hers because morning wasn't right
without them. Even though we have other shoes,
we need something thinner between us and what
others have left in intimate places: shots of semen, warm
orange juice from a carton, ancient dollop of cream cheese

or shampoo. Against sand, lint, ravelings rubbed
from everybody's hems. For a while I favored

the ballet sort, slim satin bows over my middle toes.
Perhaps I thought I'd sashay, at least be light
in the shuffle from coffee to desk, desk to toilet,

toilet to bed, bed to desk again. Valerie tells me I'll want
good ones for Scotland, tread for the castle stairs,
layers against the dank, against the ash around the hearth,
the gluey tile around the shared stool. But they hush
our moving too, and that's the main thing. Stealth.

In Berlin, mine wore a path from my door
down the windy corridor of identical doors shut
on five European men hunched, writing *very* important things.
I donned my slippers against paper clip and staple
wounds, spiky carpet, a trail of lard and vodka

the Latvian poets left from the kitchen to their rooms —
I snuck away from my desk, fixed only on the hope
that my lover might sense me coming, answer without
my knock. If he didn't, I could listen to him work:
the ditty of keys, the hum of his *du, du* on the phone,

the kiss of pages turning, breath, wind from the balcony
rifling loose paper. Posted by my bed, my slippers chose
the secret way over the two months' trail of crumbs
from bed to desk. In them I waft, not fully articulated,
not a body at all, but my own specter navigating the space

between where I should and where I'd rather be.
Against bread crumbs, cheese, blots of *erdbeeren* jam.
Against simple cold toes, against dog shit
from four countries on everyone's shoes,
against the conspicuous leavings of shared

temporary spaces. Against contact of all kinds,
because so long as our soles are swaddled in woollies,
burrowed in borrowed heat, then Lust, in his immaculate
white tux, will stay quiet, poised outside the door,
listening, but never about to knock.

The Actual Heart

Is a noise in the dark, a riot of tinny bells,
a slime slap. Grieving, it opens its red welt

and fills the air with a rib of white hurt.
Loving, it purrs a thousand soft clicks

of the throat flap. Moving, it listens
and tunes itself to itself. Is a hundred

musicians bending at once to a page
though only the oboe will take the note.

Stopping, it is an old mouse blinking
at the evening's dust motes and soft spots.

Reckoning, it roams the closed rooms
of a house where it never intended to live.

Climbing, it's a child after a bright flag
of sweetness. Spurning, it's the coarse

black hair of a woman who failed
for twenty years to say what was wanted,

who, thin lipped, furious, hurtled
what might have been part of it back at him.

No-Man's-Land

My father says there's no familiar soap in my house.
The lavender bar in the shower smells suspicious,
some frivolity of a daughter unaccustomed to male
guests. The oatmeal-apricot by the sink is a bad orange,
full of grit that snags in his palms. He calls

for my mother's stash of tiny hotel bars, white
and orthodox, with dependable deodorants and lather.
The shelf at the back of his daughter's tub is even more
upsetting, stacked with complicated female instruments
and potions, hops oil, blueing, a razor in a plastic sheath.

Her bath pillow, a blow-up scallop shell, slides against
his heels while he examines the baffling nail brush
and pumice stone. He stands naked, drooping
beneath the hot spray, missing his basement stall,
his Camay and raggedy towel. When he steps out

onto the fluff of pink, he sees his face in a mirror
ringed with gold hyenas, teeth bared over lotus flowers,
and he wonders who, besides his daughter,
can have braved that battalion of camel bone pots,
powders, tubes and wands. He calls for my mother

to help him find the right creme for his cracked
hands, to push back the frills and vials. It's all
so meticulous and his daughter still unmarried,
the city beyond the frosted window capacious,
and her desires, profuse, puzzling as her collection

of anointments. Still, he knows she's shivery, prey
to sorrows he's only heard a few of. The rest, perhaps
she doused with rose water, stoppered with jasmine.
He could ask her, later, something about the new *friend*
she's mentioned, though he knows they all evanesce

with asking. He dries his small nest of thin hair
and folds his towel carefully among the others. So much
complicitous lace, a china cat on the toilet back,
that weird basket of weeds. He moves aside a bowl
of shining stuff, digs out his Vitalis and plain black comb.

He thinks he ought to suggest something helpful, fatherly,
find a way to tell her how terrifying that tiny army of fierce
scents, those tattered blossoms bobbing like zygotes in a bottle
of bath oil. But he thinks again of the mirror beasts, all teeth
and glee, how maybe what she's after here, is hardly beauty after all.

On Being Asked What Compels Me
to Keep Making Art

Because I spent my childhood reticent, shut
up like an archive. Because I was only listening then,
perfecting my angle before I opened my mouth,
my hand, my eye. Because I couldn't sing
after years of choir practice, because I couldn't
sketch or mix a teal or throw a pot even after years
of Saturday mornings at the Art Institute, the charge
of Dr. Dietz, patient master of our splendid messes.
He meant to have a life of art himself, and got
instead these twenty kids of tidy moms, starved
for color, dirt, texture, ordinary goo, I among them
with no interest in the curve of yellow pear or dusty drape
of brocade, urns and rubber grapes. I preferred
and memorized Italian horses' twisted necks,
the foaming flanks of beasts in every battle scene.
Dr. Dietz walked us through his cherished 17th-century
sprucewood room, brought panel by panel from London,
drew shapes in air above the marble bust of Ceres,
below baroque acanthus moldings he must have packed
himself with every polished panel of that room
when the Institute was rudely moved outside of town.
We, his restless charges, believed he was the sort
of doctor who peered down throats with a paper stick,
stuck his pointed light in waxy ears and gave our mothers
meaningful looks. That he knew wax and stone,
how that bust was brought from dream, oil and pigment,
how that burnt sienna mixed two hundred years ago,
seemed not unlike the sort of thing he'd know
about a fever, itchy rash or reddened eye.
He painted clowns and Mexican children himself,
presided over the Institute collection like a surgeon
ever amazed at the magnificent and bloody workings
of a lung. I've been all my life working my way back
to those Saturday mornings with the spattered

board between my knees, the pastel dust
under my nails and smeared across one cheek.
There was something more to Dr. Dietz:
in a small town with one Dairy Queen and too many
churches, he was not one of the obvious routes
of escape. He was the doctor who might pronounce us
well or ill, who'd sigh and let us have at the wads
of wheat paste, glue and sawdust, who understood
the frail chaos of dimension and line that might,
if one were lucky, coalesce the absences
to presences again: a face, a hand, a fish, a bloody knife
on a Dutch table, a queen's tiny dog pressed to her ermined
breast. That I mistook him for a medical doctor isn't,
now, so strange a mistake — I'm that sort of doctor too —
one who hopes to bring the frowzy body back
from the expectant silence of a concert hall, from leaf
after leaf of thin gray newsprint, from the sink
of slimy clay, from the long empty curve
of white gallery walls that would have to spiral
back through snarl and grit of twenty messy centuries
to come out on the right side of creation.

Trading Love Stories in Installments,
Ruined Amphitheater, Provence

Today the indolent prologue of July, sun rattling olives
three broken Roman terraces down, a stasis
of tarnish and haze. My red beach towel fumes

on the line, and below us, a dry gorge piddles,
hooves ring the stone. Above us on a hot spar,
three shuttered houses, and a plot stirs in the white

pebbles that scorch the pads of twelve dogs,
bleaches the lavender blue. Then an itchy accompaniment
of *cigales* touches wings to feet, so you have to shout

your story at me: the crowd scene in the loony bin, the fatal
flaw that got you there: a gift of scored wrists you brought
your mother from afar. Then this lull where we could nap

in the garden of rubbled walls, or walk to the village for metal
chairs on the hosed stones. There is even a lumbering bus
we could take to the ribbon of sea, if only oleanders

weren't so thick on the path. Their hubris could blind us
like pins on golden broaches if we dared walk into them
in the dark, but in the intricate layers of afternoon,

they only wad and drop their shredded hankies
into the shrinking grass. We go nowhere but here,
you and I with our rumpled pasts, though my red

beach towel fumes on the line, all its motivations wrong;
it says nothing but that it has no end. Tell me, Olivier,
how *dénouement* might taste, better yet, intoxicate, how long

the twiggy thyme will lace the path between your place
and mine. Tell me, you who share a name with the native trees,
whether the jasmine will go on suckering with scent or fall

to tragic rust over the face of your father's house.
Tell me the American girl you loved is well and carving
widows' wishes over all her bones while she waits for you

in her tiny house in the country where I was born
and do not want to die, that you'll go back to her, simple
as she is, that you'll stay. My red beach towel fumes

on the line. Lucky and bright, but ever unwise,
it will play here after me. I need to know you'll love
this girl well and all your days, my friend, and then

the mistral's hint of menace thrilling the olives'
silver tops where you were born and cannot die,
might stay with me the rest of mine.

Cautionary Tale

for Heid Erdrich

My friend believes that people looked
a long time at the way storms took the land,
the magnificent bruising a brutish sky
could give the earth, the green's appalling swift
submission to moister air, the way the wind
could bully or breeze — and she is sure

this is how we learned the art of ravishing.
I wish I could agree with her, but I wasn't born
this far north, cannot trust how long it takes
the spring to come. It scares me, how frost
stalks night after night, how every other year,
something fails completely to go on. Gardens thin,

pavements buckle with melt, and rivers going north
forget themselves, sprawl, unlovely, muddy
perfect strangers' beds. And though I don't believe
my friend, I've accepted life alone here, stopped
making up my bed, expecting guests. I see how
my cottonwood refuses every year to dress until

the end of May, and autumn too, that one's last
to shed its underthings. The shrubs and hostas
have no shame, frill early, and the trillion tulip
wands too soon bend and quit, but the reluctance
of the trees is almost wise, or simply practiced.
If my friend is right, I cannot lend them human traits,

but take example from them as I drive along the freeway
pushing them with wishes into what they could
become, afraid of what the air has done. Ravished
by the wind and left for dead too many years to count,
those wily silver olives leaf one tight fist at a time,
so late it's hardly worth the bother for such a casual fling,

and when I push unwilling green along in the drafty
copse of my desires, I know it is afraid of something
bigger than not blooming, that my own reluctance
can't be blamed on any silly disappointing past,
but on this very landscape's bad example, dour,
dormant most of every year, all heartless self-control.

Head as Colony/Head as Landscape

after William Turnbull's Mask, *1955–56*

How easy it is to transmute the other
into yet another when we begin
to believe we need or want to see
him again: the idea that any portrait

must be mobile as a face, the globe
of the cranium at its various inclines,
each with an entirely different meaning.
Not exactly gesture or expression

but a consequence of movement. Yours,
since you're the other of the moment,
yours, since you're not actually here.
It's a matter, partly, of light, partly

of color. Green, for example, I'd make
the lower scrim of your jaw a thin green,
and turning, it might go blue a bit, but then
we'd catch the rust and mud of one eye,

since you've that opaque brown sort,
the little charcoal smear of a worry line
between, all that gives away the fact:
you too are given to ordinary anxiety.

But then we'd have to consider the frame
your arms make, outstretched as I recall
like a horizon teetering a seascape.
A different green, lighter, but grayer too

since you'd not been to the actual sea
in some weeks when I last took what we call
a look at you, added one more view
to my thickening file of yous. I'd like

to make a head of all those eggs:
how little will suggest a head,
how much load will the shape take
and still read head? I don't know

what to call the need to reconstruct
your face as a kind of seduction. Whether
it's me I'm winning over, or you, if
we could have said, after all, *looking*

or *watching.* Either way, it's a kind
of love, basic as the last strokes of yellow
Bonnard, dying, asked his nephew
to add *On the left, at the bottom*

there on the ground under the almond tree.

Mock Victorian

Most meticulous of naturalists, I know which ones
to dry and which to toss, when and how to excavate
moist buds from nests of ferns, to hang them
in my furnace closet until they shrink to scabs,
lay them stem to blossom around a silver plate.

If anyone should ask, those long-stemmed scraps
cast behind the glass once saw themselves
as Valentines, relics of an errant beau
who offered up his swaddled blooms and fled.
Most recent acquisition in the cramped museum

of female loss, this bowl of yellow petals
who remember falling from their wands, a view
of water, city where I went to harvest summer
and a boy. Now these crimps love their dust
as much as any of the rest, and my good furnace blasts

the last of rose sweat from their air. Tenuous as flowers are,
they will, I know, outlive the sentiment they ride
into my rooms while I wait (not patiently at all)
for the next season's root of reason (I need only one)
to clear the shelves and bowls of this year's husks.

Not one, even of my female friends, dares remark
the oddity of my collection, the spooky army
of miniatures that frame my family of evaporated lusts.
No new guest would ever ask significance for fear
he might appear himself in sacristy. Even I can't touch

the paper curls, blessed and weird as the dressed-up
bones of an abbey's most beloved monk, fray of lace
beneath his skull, to which (to whom?) a pretty innocent
must always pray. Bones, petals — better the flattened
blue snake I took from Rich's place in August,

sharing now the shrine with two white deer toes,
a gnarled turtle claw, disemboweled bouquets
from lovers more remote — meaning blissful nothing now;
what survived was only baby's breath, *weeds*
my mother warns, that will erupt in insects

(natural matter in the house isn't right). If I'd like,
she'll lend her clot of rubber pears and grapes,
but I'd rather see my scavengings alive again,
rinsed in living oils and scents, all of them
plump, potent, ruddy and returned to me

with the unbelievably sweet sanctimony
(I know it well) that sniggers and marvels
at the heat in the heart of every about-to-be-given
last (but only later understood as such) kiss.

Véritable Laguiole

Now that I see I'll lose them all, I understand the trademark
on the blade she gave me, blade he must have told her
I desired. He knew it had the power to part us — the way
he'd gifted her with parting from the German girl.

If you give a knife, he says, *you have to take a coin,*
or someone's cut from you. He gave her *Laguiole* in June,
the finest he could find, and the girl she loved was packed
and gone before October's rains. These haunting knives

ubiquitous in all the shops, famous French *cadeaux,*
Napoleon's iconic bee alight on every silver handle,
are carted off in boxed authentic sets by hoards
of unsuspecting tourists, those they grace them with

soon severed from their lives. Just last week I stopped
with him to have his pocket version honed and shined.
It was a gift I'd made to him, antique but sturdy piece
unearthed beneath my roses. They do their work

too well, these flashy little lancets. The priciest etched
with toy Lucretias, she who bore a rape and turned a dagger
through her heart. Now he borrows mine, demonstrates exactly
how to gut a little dog: *blade up, thrust deeply just below the ribs,*

pull upward toward your chin, ripping clean from balls
to throat. By the time he's thought to bite your wrist,
his heart is on the floor, his jaws unhinged, the hard
charms of his teeth, your souvenirs. I take back the knife,

my own from her, shut it in its velvet pouch. He saved me
once before from buying *Laguioles* as gift: *The coins,*
he said, *aren't always safe,* and I could almost trust *care*
was what he had in mind. She who wields a knife must

have instruction in the art of ire, beware beguiling gifts
which first appear mere instruments for opening fruit,
gutting trout or gouging garden dirt from fingernails.
When we're given weapons, something deep beneath desire

to give a useful gift, maybe get one in return, must thrill
the valiant giver. He thinks of how, untutored, but seduced
by jut and glint, the veritable gift of sharpness in our hands,
we're apt to turn the unforgiving points upon ourselves.

Panorama Place

Her view to the sea has all but vanished,
and she fears her heart is breaking the house
to bits, seeping under the tiles. Last night, a cracking
below like a vandal's tools on the doors. Or an animal,

she thought, leaping up in the moonless dark,
the salt of lights on the way to the sea flung
in what might be mist, might be smoke.
Things burn here if they're not kept green.

She stood at the top of the stairs, listened,
but the breaking had stopped. Whatever
she was dreaming stopped too. Perhaps
she would find it dead in the morning, a bird,

a rat, one of the dozens of village cats
who've come back since she's here. Yesterday,
she picked as many peaches as she could, some
so soft they pulped in her hands, gave the whole

flat to the cat woman who comes daily at five
with her flashing gold tooth, her can of reeking meat
for the fat, fawn-colored Grizzou. *I don't believe
in cutting them,* says the old woman. Only the fattest

is getting fed. The others wait. One chews on a leaf.
There are too many peaches for me. I am alone,
she tells the cat woman in her baby French. The rest
she doesn't know how to say: swollen, the tree,

its tiny spine bent, the branches staggering.
She would also like to ask the cat woman
about the breaking in the night, the tiles like eggshells
underfoot in the morning. Either the mountain

is moving, or water is moving under the house.
It's not her house, and she worries that her heart
did this. Her late heart. Now, too early to call anyone,
she makes the coffee, goes out into the garden

where everything is bright and brittle. Sees him
there at her gate, the most beautiful man in the village,
Fabrice, waiting for his dog to finish. Later
they'll come with hoses before she dresses,

men who wash the streets, push the detritus along
the warm cobbles, wash it down the old ramparts,
down into the Barbary figs and aloes. She's stretching
like a cat when she sees the beautiful man and he her.

He doesn't speak English. He thinks she doesn't speak
French at all, and she lets him think that, because she
doesn't want talk. She is still in her nightgown, pink
and flimsy, barefoot, her hair a mop. And the floor

is groaning behind her, busting up. The sunlight
is weak. His eyes are weak and blue and narrow,
and she flees his stare, into the dark house,
the fracturing floor, the double-image aftermath

of insomnia. Peaches again for breakfast. Damp
bread. It has to be water, she thinks, under the floor.
The sea which she can no longer see has somehow
risen up through the rock, through the mountain.

Under her feet, the shells of the tiles breaking up.
Terror. Later, dressing, there is also blood.
Not from a wound as she wishes. It's the heart
again, swelling, telling her there is really no child

after all. The most beautiful man in the village
is gone when she looks out through the roses again.
It was natural to walk his dog there. Maybe
he had been there every day. Maybe he was looking

for her. Once he had spoken to her in French,
something about her eyes. He didn't know
if she understood him. *Yours also,* she had answered.
They say he has loved all possible women in the village,

the region, and soon he is leaving for Corsica,
the island which lies out there in the invisible sea.
They say also that he belonged all his youth
to a very famous, very rich man, and when

he'd become a man himself, his lover turned him
back to women, for whom he was still eager, still
with a boy's wonder at how they're made. She's no more
than a new mystery. The village is small. She could

have said *Bonjour.* She could have said *salut, ça va.*
Bonne journée. Comment va tu? But there was the heart
knocking on the floor, blood knocking on the gates
of her, all tousle and despair. She didn't even see

his dog, only assumed him. She could have
invited them into the garden simply with a look,
could have lifted her gown, given him, there and then
the body that was busy betraying her, the body

that couldn't manage to keep even one of the tiny
scribbles. The most beautiful man in the village,
she thinks, maybe in the whole South of France,
and he's giving them away, his genes,

like chances on a prize, like peaches.

Cartography with Crows

for Christina Viragh

This year's loss left for Madrid on Monday with a woman
who betrayed me, who took the man I'd charted
for myself (and only incidentally for her) as fabulous
coast, secret springs, fallen stars and wet moss.

Even as they climbed into the plane's dim belly against
the glare of midwinter's midday, I heard crows,
first earth noise of any cold city coming back, omnivorous
scavengers, burly and stout as charred bricks.

*Notorious nest plunderers, they weed out the weak
and the feeble,* unfold my way back to a house
at the edge of Berlin, their bald caws crossing out
my petty disappointments, until I hear it raining in Rome

where a woman I met in the excavated basement
of the Gestapo headquarters and must now trust as much
as myself, doesn't yet understand why she scribbles my name
on the page, hoping my silence means movement,

and not its ugly twin, stasis, has found and closed my mouth.
Lemons nod on the trees in her garden, encumbered
with Roman rain pooling and pulling, its maddeningly patient
erasures, and here is her letter arrived and now dry, but fragile

and rippled as anything once doused, dropped in a puddle,
but saved by her smart permanent ink, her familiar
scrawl still winged, though its black alphabet's been bled
to sepia, while its thinned spine is oddly blue, evidence

that she folded it dry, half-finished, went off of a morning
when doves huddled under her eaves, perhaps bought
the fistful of squid, some lime, the white wine we liked
from the green bottle shaped like a fish, tried a star fruit

at the market lit by the white flanks of Bernini's steeds,
and looked up at the whirl and arc of a flock of shadows
before turning south, thinking, *birds have colonized all parts
of the world*. Rain must have lifted the starch from her shirt,

dampened pages she'd packed from the Hungarian tale
she struggled to bring into German. I'm sure she couldn't
decide where she'd work, returned to the garden,
though it was too wet, the lemons not really in season,

and the backs of her books bled against the wood
of the table where the trees had wept all night.
Instead of work, she found herself listening to my heart's
petty flutter and stall in a cold house with a thin view

of a peevish American river, found herself retracing
the way we both had charted the alarming assembly
of crows filling the blanks of elms by the Wannsee
every morning and every evening, as the unanswerable

admonition they were: to go home. We were tourists
and women alone in that place, agreed to tea and tears
when we climbed out of the "Topography of Terror"
together. Now our letters are blackened and raucous

with the articulate rumpus of all manner of plunder,
but I am still learning how to read beyond the loud *loss-loss*
of my trivial griefs, how the *caw-caws* are also a map of larger
dangers, how to hear from whence those harder harms come.

Collecting Ashes after an Estrangement

Half a mile to the ridge recently cleared
and burned, I go to scoop with my broken
shard of terra-cotta pot, the charred nuggets

of what was a wood, now gold to me
in grocery bags. As I dig and dump, sort
the glass and metal out, I consider how

this whisper dust will heal my grudging dirt.
I haul it home, my bags of darkness,
bags of ash, elemental stuff I've filched

from God knows whom to plant my borrowed
piece of France. The white parts sift
with weightlessness. I rake it in, this not

yet finished matter. Wet, it blackens up
my dirt, makes a creamy glue to bind
the crumbled clods of peat, root,

pine rot, twigs and cones, weed dross,
mulch and molds. She's recommended this
as remedy, my friend an ocean and half

another continent away, who calls to see
if I'm OK, not gone too deep beneath
the local avalanche of factiousness,

a bit of dissonance, and residue of spite.
They are completely crazy people,
understand, she warns. *Will yourself superior.*

She holds me up, the voice from somewhere far,
and tells me most exactly how to make
my garden well. I know nothing, never did,

of how to keep things green, but her instructions
get me through. *This is how,* she says
to cut the acid in the soil: ashes. *Love you.*

Love you too, am sending seeds. This way
we keep my sweet peas, timid ladies (Royal
Mix) moving, gracious, aiming at the sun.

The Many Faucets of Love

The young man in my poetry class who insists
he's writing about love (though the images
are of a murder scene, a whore's boudoir),
won't budge. His intentions (*oh love, glum
love*) must prevail. Rather than go with the happy
accident, he wants to know how to make it say

what he thinks he feels, writes that the "voice
of love" is his interest here, that he wants
to speak of "its many faucets." Yes, *faucets* —
as in what drips, what sometimes freezes.
My young charge, he wouldn't like this metaphor
I'm making, and he wouldn't be sure why —

but he can't be all of twenty yet, and my forty
gives me edge, a whole drawer of sashes, gaudy
and slippery as blood: "irony" will filter in tomorrow
next week or year — anytime's too soon, and even
when it does, he won't know what to call it —
only that it's wrong and much to be resisted.

He's been reading Wordsworth, and Coleridge's
earliest lyrics; Byron and Blake are problematic,
of course, but Keats is really tops, and Shelley
can be forced to fit. Shakespeare's sonnets
have enough of what he's looking for, so all
of what he's not can be ignored. The *r*

on his *romanticism* is still in lower case; the *R*
on mine writ larger now, but even as I tell him
his poem's gone down a road he really doesn't want,
I know mine follow suit: all the *mighty fountains*
in my house still drip and freeze, though with something less
than *tumult,* and however hard I try to think of *facets,*

eight or a dozen crisp angles on the dim thing
we're calling *love,* I too am stuck with drippy taps,
sinks messy as murder scenes. I too refuse
to turn away from that hardy cliché, all that crude
wailing, that fabulous vision replete with damsel (i.e., me),
dulcimer, gone-done-me-wrong lover, and much wet distress.

One Moon View of Puget Sound

I loved a boy and green water dared near my feet,
roses fell apart in my hands, stones turned their troll
shoulders and said *go ahead, stumble.*

And I did. All the green days I combed my straw-colored hair
and patted my eyes with creme. All the warm days I hid
my dragons in a fen of remembered trees.

We went to the edge of his mother, but I wasn't invited
to drink. He washed my ribs with a long hand, dressed me,
tied my shoes upside down and tight.

I loved a boy in a house that wasn't mine. The sun bled most
beautifully going off, and stars bounced like unstrung
beads on the porch floor. I gave him views given to me.

We loved a dog that wasn't ours, pulled limp sheets
above our heads against slithers of light, skin that wasn't
ours, pillows and dishes and lettuce and basement steps

that weren't ours, windows and closets and high ceilings
in deep pink rooms, green bricks, white cups full of being
not ours. The animals belong to a child younger than all the years

between us. Somewhere a clock I never found still ticks.
Comes a time in loving when there's nothing to tell, but that the light
was right, and the rain behaved. I loved a boy and the gulls wept

inside a fog. Nothing happened except that I couldn't remember
the name of the flower I loved best in that city, hydrangea,
hydrangea, hydrangea, blues and violets so unnatural

it hurt to see them swelling at the steps and railings, holding
the hills up. Salmon thrashed through us toward the streams
of their birth, gaping red slashes where they'd leapt

over rocks and piers and come back down behind
where they were going, scales and fish flesh streaming away
in the backwash. Purple coins of the money bush.

I loved a boy because there was a long bandage of water
and dark enough for me to smell everything again. His father
said he knew a story like this, and it was good.

He must have made Spokane by noon. Between love
and lust is a green fish, swifter than ever you'd guess,
a wish of wings. I'll go home to Russian olives,

books and eager autumn, but I cannot look into the face
of anyone young without hearing freighters scraping piers, a door
nosed open by a cat who wants to walk on that mist.

I loved a boy and nothing changed. I knew already
what tenderness was, how breath collects behind the knees
and two bodies begin to need different skins.

My hands are brown as leather and not new. I turn
them palm up so they match anyone's. Come now,
I'll dress you for all the days ahead. I'll hold

your feet like heavy blooms about to fall apart.
I loved a boy and lost nothing except momentum.
Ferries polish away the fog and the islands hunker

while something, *is it wind?,* rocks the wicker rocker.
A house here and there blinks out of the fog, and I can tell you
this which was once secret: I've wanted anyone's child all along.

Charm

Sunday evening dumpster find, these tiny slippers,
size one, were once among the finest Paris
had to offer, now tossed still swaddled
in their snowy tissues, tucked in glossy ruby boxes.

He likes and wants the gold-embellished cartons,
but the shoes, I urge, seem takable too, itty-bitty boats,
pointed toes, needle heels for toy French lady feet.
He packs them underarm, black suede pumps,

a lacework beige, the leopard slings. Sooty margins,
oil of some outmoded woman's sole smeared
against the arches, pressure of the miles
she's logged rubbed into the heels. I convince him

that they may, if nothing else, amuse the girl
who waits for him with whom I'm making sport
of raiding dumpsters. Only half an hour ago,
he tried again to tempt me, sun-lazy, silly,

quoted me his version of some clever Oscar Wilde:
The only difference between eternal passion
and caprice — caprice lasts longer. And yes,
the shoes regale the girl, exactly as I promised.

They almost fit her too, the leopard skins she likes,
though she'd rather make an artwork of them,
hangs each cradle from its needle heel on a string
beside his door, perhaps to ward off poachers on the man.

They pitch toward their tips in an eternal circle,
tangling, then untangling from their tether. And she
who bought these shoes years ago in Paris,
must, just this morning, have plucked the ice-pick

heels, said *time for something sensible,* and tossed
them in the *poubelle.* She of the blue-hairs who haunt
the Boulevard de Lattre Sunday afternoons, three
to a bench with poodles, and the gentleman

they share leaning on his polished cane, complaining
of the taxes, trading tortures for their vines, wayward
wisteria that gouges mortar from their cottage walls,
needs its roots notched, its tendrils trained on wires overhead.

As she suspends the shoes above us now, the girl's
abundant breasts crescendo in her cotton tee, tip her
toward a milky sweetness even I can smell and revel in.
I lean as close to her as he does, approving of her shape.

She fills each pointy toe with wands of yellow bloom.
They twirl toward their cargo of distances traversed,
and in their prows a crowd of weightless wild flowers
enjoys the ride. Only yesterday these castoffs were

still cherished souvenirs. She wanted something special
in which to meet a lover years ago, she who now
must take her tea alone, who doesn't know we hang
her hopes, a kitschy entertainment, a teasing

of the air. I turn to her whose feet they almost fit,
the pleasure of her nearness set adrift in my head,
my senses tipping with the burden of her youth, whirling
with the furls of wild weed, and feel the heart's impulsive

purchase taking up its rightful second life as charm.

Where the Nots Go

for Hannelore Jüterbock

She remembers how it felt to fall in love at five.
The boy was *beautiful* and *great* and never knew
she loved. This is how our meals always start:
we rehearse the German schoolboy over olives,

nuts, the first glass of wine. *I understand not*
men is the way she proudly hands the story off
to me. I try to take her cue, remember that she's German
and for that our rules are different: *sex* a word

she knows but studiously avoids. I ask about her feeling
for the Russian; she about my Native beau. I try to understand
that consummation's not the finish line for her,
but when my turn comes up, I have too many options:

crush and *lust, affair* and *fling, flirtation,* simple *woo.*
She's offered her compendium complete — fifty years
of fairy tales held up with only *greats* and *loves,* while I'm still
picking through my terms, *lust* being one that even Roget

doesn't deign to index, and anyway for her, *lust*
is merely *pleasure,* goes with *garten* not with men.
She never spoke *to* any on her list, only *of,*
and I could say the same, the lovely avocado salad

having just arrived. Yes, mine were all sweet ideas once,
though now and then I couldn't help but listen
to my blood: it demanded ordinary things like sweat
and noisy springs. I've violated story protocol by veering

from the mythic track; she brings me back by asking
if I know my Plato, *Two faces on one head,*
you must remember this? What our meal tonight
is for, and why she's picked this place, *Au coin*

du feu. She thinks I can be cured of doubt, wants me
to rehearse them all again, tag them by their toes, *loves*
and *nots*. My pink and perfect headless trout arrives,
and I admit to thrilling at her poet neighbor, concede

the lyric boy, the one before, the one not yet, and one
who follows me to every country Sundays with his bargain
calling card. *But the great one,* she insists, *you want not
have it?,* at which our waiter reappears, an enigmatic apple

in his hand. He peels it while teasing her in German, declaring
me desirable in French, and going back to English
for our choices of dessert. He's let us know he's onto us
and wants to play along. *You are a bachelor?,* he asks me

pouring our champagne, but my German friend,
she doesn't know that word, hears instead and asks,
He want be your butler? Before she sees she's made a joke,
he's writhing on the floor, and all the English speakers

crammed against the cellar walls unravel into laughter,
while she's incredulous, uncomprehending, slightly hurt,
still bent on healing me with Plato, and sadly, she concludes,
I understand not what can mean this man.

Lingua Franca

The telephone rings at 2 A.M. and German pours out
of a machine near the window, spills over the terrace,
down the road the Romans built and into the River Loup.
Frogs listen, pretend to answer. Someone imagines

the woman who owns the house listening, speaks to
and for her, waits, in case she's groping for her robe,
stumbling down the medieval stairs, pushing
her blond braid back over her shoulder. Then

danke, tcheuss, rewind. . . . Someone has not imagined
an American alone in the upper room, reading late,
a biography of a Russian woman, savoring it,
because after it, there is nothing else of substance

in English to read. Too long out of her mother
tongue, even her own parents don't recognize
her voice on the phone. Here, they take her for
German because her sentences are labored, the verbs

too late. There is only one more book in the box,
but she knows it so well she doesn't read it anymore,
only carries it, spineless, from country to country.
It is Rilke, and she will not share it. The frogs

in the gorge know everything now: French, of course,
Italian, German, her particular English. Her fake
Southern accent which she hauls out to entertain
the Europeans. They look at her mouth when she does it

as if the lips might be doing something visible,
as if there is suddenly a new person in her body.

II

She tries to imagine what it would be like to take up
another language so ardently endearments occurred in it.

For her, it wouldn't be French. It would have to be
a language *in* which, rather than *with* which one had
fallen in love. Only today there was the problem of what
to put on the envelope: *Autriche,* the loveliest of all

the possibilities, but what would they do with that
in Graz? *Österreich* then, though Marseilles may
be confused, indignant, refuse to deliver. *Austria,*
most likely to help it find the way, but also absurd.

She wrote all three. Secretly pleased she'd been able
to do all the talking for him. She had ordered his food,
got him directions, prices, bits of history, toilets.
For once, he had to ask her helplessly for words.

But there came an afternoon. They were flushed,
dusty, had been driving all day around the same mountain,
Cézanne's, lost from even their own tongues. Only the rumor
of blue rock. Dare I say it, *she pretended not to understand.*

After so much struggle to be understood. Immediately,
she was sorry, tried to give him a gift: something simple,
something elegant enough to keep. Touching him,
which he did understand. He took a stone in the shape

of the mountain to remember the mountain. She took three
poppies to remember the shape his mouth had on *Victoire.*

III

They both saw the names of the towns on the map,
but when he took them in his mouth, she no longer
recognized them: French towns, Austrian sounds.
There were circles on the map. He'd drawn them

carefully, with half-schilling pieces. Except for the circles
she had no idea where they were going. Three graves.
Max Ernst they never found. Camus was there
but his marker so eaten by weather they almost

missed it. The mistral had come again, and her skirt
was too short. She waited in the car till he found it,
came back to get her. Chagall was last and easiest.
His place sunny, tasteful. The only one she wished

to photograph, the lover's silhouette on the white stone,
a bird etched lightly under his shadow. He seemed
about to cry, but whether his feeling was for Chagall
or for her whom he would leave that day, she did not

know. It was an askable question, but she didn't.
She is still trying to get the story of his childhood
straight. What might it mean to drive a thousand
kilometers to see a lover for three days. To have also

the desire to visit, each day, the grave of a famous man?
He says *I will this* when he means *I want.*

IV

The answering machine speaks French, *il y a trois messages.*
One is in English, an invitation for her. One is in French,

and she listens twice before she knows they are speaking
also to her. *Pick up your photos when you like.* The other,

the German one, is not for her, but she's awake,
looks up from Tsvetaeva in Berlin, Pasternak's
horsy face, the beautiful eyes of the weak husband,
and listens the way one who loves Chopin but cannot

play the piano listens. Ardently. Separating herself
from the distasteful evening endured in English,
the American man who tried to seduce her, tried
to make her let go of the distant nocturnes. *Tant pis,*

she says to him under her breath. *Gehen Sie.* She loves
pushing them away like this in languages they don't know,
believes that even if you never learn to speak the patois,
you can dream in it, hear the notes falling in another room,

another fear or shape or prayer. One night in a bar,
she'd looked a ruffian right in the eye, let him see
how she also noticed those disagreeable beads
of the too much he'd had to drink breaking out

on his temples. Dog. *Cluatutta, faltegenetto,* she'd said
to him as if he ought to understand. *Teessot. Clemmo.*
Asshole. With urgency. With scorn. *You understand perfectly,*
said her straight spine, *there's a world locked in my mouth,*

and it's not yours.

Prévert's Peaches

Notre Père qui êtes aux cieux
Restez-y
Et nous nous resterons sur la terre

Appeared on the tree, an accident of abundance,
a revelry that carried limbs to the ground,

but gently, so nothing spoiled. The tree came
with Prévert's house, his dizzying view, history,

so we ate of it straight from the branches, freeing
the warm gobs, nearly sin, still in the act of ripening

in our mouths. *Eat quite everything you see,* she said,
handing me the key. Because I was still warm from love

beyond my reach, scribbled with that yellow orange
she favored lighting ramparts by the sea, she gathered me,

bruised only under the skin, not much, not visibly. No place
of me for birds to get in. Because I'd loved so stupidly

and thoroughly, she offered refuge in the poet's house,
his peaches sunk in syrup seep, his blue view languishing

all the way to the coast, where the sea, marveling at its own
capacity for ease, naps the afternoon, pearly as the milk

toweled from my skin after I'd said what I had to say:
Wir müssen keine Kinder machen. Only she knew

I hadn't meant it. She who had decided I simply ought
to make the child by myself. She'd saved a river once

by painting it, several dozen mongrel dogs, four broken chairs
Matisse once owned. Now she hands it over to me whole,

the lavish harvest, house, and all her mended stories.
She nearly saved an island outside Venice, will save it yet,

once headed up the Munich Greens. She makes me nettle soup,
tells me all about the young Albanian she rescued from a camp,

the others kept me young; he was the one who made me old.
She's made herself a life in cadmiums and light, teaches me

how to larder sweetness with seeing far. We gave ourselves
everything our mothers thought that men should and would

provide, land, houses, what authority there was. She gave
herself rooftops and sea blocks, sky smear and boat slash,

this door unfolded on the sun, the tree outside, its branches
ridden to the ground with helios, rose madder, mars and coral.

Three times she married, and never once for love. We laugh,
wet mouths stuffed with Prévert's colossal sweets,

their honey jotted on our wrists. We swallow fruit
and azure air as if we've always known what we know now,

what drives our lush capacity for greed. The more
we give ourselves, the more we can afford the heart's caprice.

Eat, she says, inviting me to take the painter's chair,
another Prévert peach, *eat quite everything you see.*

Notes

"*Clarté:* Staël at Antibes": Picasso Museum, Château Grimaldi, Antibes. On the museum's top floor, in what was Picasso's studio in 1946, works by Nicholas de Staël, who lived and worked in Antibes from September 1954 until his death by suicide in 1955, are currently displayed. Hans Hartung, also has work in the Picasso Museum. Quoted portions from Tate Gallery Exhibition Catalogue, *Nicholas de Staël,* London, 1981:"Staël a Quarter of a Century Later," Pierre Granville, and "Nicholas de Staël," Denys Sutton. Italic portions from selected letters of Staël to Douglas Cooper (January 1955) and Jacques Dubourg (June 1952). René Char, 1907–1988, French poet with whom de Staël collaborated in 1952.

"After an Evening with Mickey Rourke, I Pick Up Petrarch": Translations and descriptions of Petrarch quoted from *Selected Sonnets, Odes and Letters: Petrarch,* Thomas G. Bergin, Editor. (AHM Publishing: Arlington Heights, Illinois, 1966). *Year of the Dragon* (1985) staring Mickey Rourke and John Lone, directed by Michael Cimino.

"*La Création*":"Die Schöpfung," an oratorio by Joseph Haydn (1732–1809).

"Sundays When Their Laps Were Full of Light": Alain of Lille (1114?–1203?), Flemish theologian and philosopher. Quoted in *Lélia:The Life of George Sand,* André-Maurois, translated by Gerard Hopkins, London: Jonathan Cape (1952)."Anacampserote": quoted portions from Joseph Shipley, *Dictionary of Word Origins,* New York: The Philosophical Library (1945).

"Three Begonias":"Women believe . . .":Joseph Joubert (1754–1824)."She ought to love . . .": Eugene Lambert to Emile Aucante, 1852, both quoted in *Lélia:The Life of George Sand.*

"Head as Colony/Head as Landscape": Title and earlier italics from *William Turnbull, Exhibition Catalogue* by Richard Morphet, Tate Gallery, London, 1973. The final lines are from Annette Vallant's *Bonnard,* Thames on Hudson, London, 1966.

"Cartography with Crows":"Topography of Terror," a documentary exhibition of numerous terror sites of the Nazi era. The exhibition is housed in a cellar of the former Gestapo Headquarters uncovered in 1987 in the Prince Albert District of Berlin. Wannsee, suburb of Berlin, site of the Wannsee

Conference where "the final solution" meetings took place. Gianlorenzo Bernini (1598–1680), Italian artist and sculpltor. Some of the italicized phrases in the poem are from *The Audubon Society Field Guide to North American Birds* by Miklos D. F. Udvardy, Knopf, 1977.

"Lingua Franca": Montagne de Sainte Victoire to the east of Aix-en-Provence, where Cézanne lived at the end of his life. Albert Camus, buried in Lourmarin. Marc Chagal, buried in St. Paul-de-Vence, France.

"Prévert's Peaches": Jacques Prévert (1900–1977) lived some years in Tourrettes-sur-Loup, a hill village in the South of France. Henri Matisse (1869–1954) lived in nearby Vence. The epigraph is from Prévert's poem "Pater Noster," "Our Father who art in heaven / Stay there / And we'll stay here on earth," translated by Lawrence Ferlinghetti, *The Random House Book of 20th Century Poetry* (New York: Vintage, 1984).

LESLIE ADRIENNE MILLER's previous collections include *Yesterday Had a Man in It, Ungodliness,* and *Staying Up For Love.* She has won a number of prizes and awards, including the Loft McKnight Award of Distinction, a National Endowment for the Arts Fellowship in Poetry, the PEN Southwest Discovery Award, two Writers-at-Work Fellowships, a Pushcart Prize, the Billee Murray Denny Award in Poetry, and a number of prizes from literary magazines, including the Anne Stanford Poetry Prize, the Strousse Award from *Prairie Schooner,* and the *Nebraska Review* Poetry Award. She has also held fellowships and residencies in Switzerland, Spain, France, Scotland, Germany, and Indonesia. Currently Associate Professor of English at the University of Saint Thomas in Saint Paul, Minnesota, she holds degrees in creative writing and English from Stephens College, the University of Missouri, the Iowa Writers' Workshop, and the University of Houston.

This book has been set in Bembo, a typeface produced
by Monotype in 1929 and based on a roman cut at Venice
by Francesco Griffo in 1495.
Book design by Wendy Holdman
Composition by Stanton Publication Services, Saint Paul, Minnesota
Manufactured by Bang Printing on acid-free paper

Graywolf Press is a not-for-profit, independent press. The books we publish include poetry, literary fiction, and cultural criticism. We are less interested in best-sellers than in talented writers who display a freshness of voice coupled with a distinct vision. We believe these are the very qualities essential to shape a vital and diverse culture.

Thankfully, many of our readers feel the same way. They have shown this through their desire to buy books by Graywolf writers; they have told us this themselves through their e-mail notes and at author events; and they have reinforced their commitment by contributing financial support, in small amounts and in large amounts, and joining the "Friends of Graywolf."

If you enjoyed this book and wish to learn more about Graywolf Press, we invite you to ask your bookseller or librarian about further Graywolf titles; or to contact us for a free catalog; or to visit our award-winning web site that features information about our forthcoming books.

We would also like to invite you to consider joining the hundreds of individuals who are already "Friends of Graywolf" by contributing to our membership program. Individual donations of any size are significant to us: they tell us that you believe that the kind of publishing we do *matters*. Our web site gives you many more details about the benefits you will enjoy as a "Friend of Graywolf"; but if you do not have online access, we urge you to contact us for a copy of our membership brochure.

www.graywolfpress.org

Graywolf Press
2402 University Avenue, Suite 203
Saint Paul, MN 55114
Phone: (651) 641-0077
Fax: (651) 641-0036
E-mail: wolves@graywolfpress.org

Other Graywolf titles you might enjoy are:

Still Life with Waterfall
by Eamon Grennan

Bellocq's Ophelia
by Natasha Trethewey

Antebellum Dream Book
by Elizabeth Alexander

My Favorite Apocalypse
by Catie Rosemurgy

Feeling as a Foreign Language: The Good Strangeness of Poetry
by Alice Fulton